THANK YOU

Amirah Palmer, Publisher

A skater, visionary, serial entrepreneur, and the CEO of Sk8rz Konnect, Amirah Palmer is a decorated U.S. Army Veteran, international best selling author, graduate of the University of Maryland, and passionate about volunteering and helping others in the community.

Thank you for supporting Sk8rz Konnect, as we continue to bring you the excitement and the family love that is rampant in the world of skating.

As a platform to connect the passion of skate culture, we highlight the skills and artistry of the forms of skating: roller, ice, and skateboarders around the world.

Through our publications, *The Evolution of Skating* and *Phenomenal Sk8rz*, we collaborate with our tribe of skaters to take you on a journey of sorts, detailing the introduction, acceptance, growth and mastering of the art and skill. It is the "Evolution" of the skater. In their own words, you will read stories of skaters legendary and new, deejays, event coordinators, videographers, skate critics, rink owners—national and international.

PHENOMENAL SK8RZ

April/May 2022

EDITOR-IN-CHIEF

Amirah Palmer

GUEST EDITOR

Lynna Davis

GRAPHIC/INTERIOR DESIGN

Jessica Tilles
TWASolutions.com

PUBLISHER

SK8RZ Konnect
3695 Highway 6 South, Suite 114
Sugar Land, Texas 77478
eMail: publisher@sk8rzkonnect.com
Website: www.sk8rzkonnect.com

PURCHASE ISSUES

Quantities may be purchased at www.sk8rzkonnect.com and Ingram Book Group.
Individual copies may be purchased at Amazon.com, BarnesandNoble.com,
and wherever publications are sold.

ISBN: 978-1-7378461-5-4

TABLE OF CONTENTS

Lynna Davis
aka Lynna Moving Star, New York

Guest Editor

Greetings, royal sk8 family, friends and wonderful people!

I'm extremely honored to be involved with the premier edition of *Phenomenal Sk8rz*.

As a passionate lover for the world of entertainment and an artist, I wake up every morning, thanking God for life daily. Then I take a deep breath and think where will I sk8 today? I'm in love with roller skating and the joy it brings. When I asked God to just let me roll through life, He certainly did and sk8ing has been a blessing to many, in and out of the sk8 world.

I've choreographed and booked many sk8ing events—Avicii, Trolls, Cynthia Riley, Elie Tahari, Abc Localish, Reuters, and the list goes on.

Roller skating is making a huge difference in the world today as it has in the past. The pandemic has led many to look for a healthy addiction. Roller skating is a real healer, mentally physically, creatively, spiritually and financially.

Roller skating has taken over the entertainment media by storm. Commercials, TV, TikTok, and sk8 documentaries lead the roll.

All sk8ers are looking forward for more rinks to open. We all know that Manhattan, the Bronx, and Brooklyn are truly long overdue, since the closing of Roxy Roller Rink, Sk8 22, and Empire. All we talk about are rinks opening again in major cities. Whoever hits the lottery first, it's a go.

Sk8rz Konnect has set a platform for many sk8rz to comfortably share their passion for roller skating. I met Amirah Palmer, who is the founder of Sk8rz Konnect, on the set of the recording of JUST/Skat/theDocumentary. Amirah loves sk8ing and all the excitement that comes with it. Meeting sk8 artists like me and many others have episodes to share for a lifetime. *The Evolution of Skating* creates a unique unlimited outstanding platform. Amirah You're Incredible. I am so happy that I was invited to come aboard.

Being a part of this huge sk8 world, sk8ting has helped and healed many. Sk8ers have found a big relief and release being able to share their stories.

Sk8 artists are motivated and inspired to capitalize on their personal skills and lifestyles.

Many sk8ers all over the world have become extremly popular and maintain professional careers.

Amirah Palmer, ThaQueen, Mz Phenomenal Herself, thank you for opening the roller skating doors for the world to see.

Facebook: lynna.davis
Instagram: lynnamovingstar

Edna Davoll

New York and Columbia, South Carolina

What is your skate style?

I enjoy various skate styles. I'm very comfortable with line dance skating, free style, slow walk, and partner skating. I am always eager to learn and join in with other skaters' styles.

What is your skate setup?

Edea boot with Giotto Rolline plate.

What is your favorite skate song?

"I've Got to Use My Imagination" by Gladys Knight & the Pips

The very first time you laced up, how did you feel?

Lace up? What's that? (smile) The very first time I put on skates, I used a skate key. Yes! I placed my foot into the skates and adjusted the sides using a skate key to tighten the skate to my shoe. I was excited, nervous, anxious and afraid all at once. My very first location wasn't in a rink, but in my now sister-in-law's house basement. We had to be extremely careful because in the middle of the floor was a potbelly stove and we had to be careful not to fall onto the stove and get burned. I loved it and was instantly hooked!

In my early teens, over Christmas vacation, all of the kids would gather on the only paved road in the neighborhood. Yes, we only had one paved road. We would meet and skate all day. That would be the highlight of our vacation time together.

Somewhere along the way, I became busy with life and quit skating. In 1975, a good friend invited me to Waverly Place Village Rink in Greenwich Village, New York City. That rink was about as big as a living room. But the fire was back in my soul and my love for skating was instantaneous. I knew it was something that I really loved doing. The Village Wizards were a skate team out at that time, doing amazing things and I wanted to do what they did…they were so motivating. That night I skated in rentals, but the very next day I purchased white Chicago skates. I used them for about three months before purchasing my first pair of Riedells with the dance Snyder plate.

What are your hidden superpowers, something crazy unique—secret power—that others don't know about you?

I have to give all honor to God for His greatness. For he's given me a superb immune system and my cell repair is top notch. It is my opinion, speaking from a biochemical aspect, that these secret powers have enabled my body to heal faster; they have minimized my illnesses; I don't seem to age as fast; my hair hasn't fallen out; and I'm constantly amazed by the sheer strength of my wellness, both physically and mentally. I can personally testify to roller skating's many health benefits, i.e., normalized blood pressure, burning calories, strengthening muscles, and social interactions. Even after my hip replacement, I was back on my skates in three months. I enhance God's favor by eating healthy and exercising daily. I'm not perfect, nor do I want to boast about my good fortune, but being healthy makes me happy and allows me to enjoy roller skating to the utmost! After every skate session, I feel like I can skate for another two or three hours. I don't know if it's the love that I feel when I'm on the wood, or if it's the blessing of good health. Maybe it's both. But as long as I am blessed, for as long as I can..."I'm leaving it all on the wood!"

How has skating impacted your life?

Prior to roller skating, I was engaged in several hobbies, including, but not limited to, bike riding, line dancing, snow skiing, assisting teaching gym classes, hula hooping and volunteering for the NY Marathon and the NY Century Bike Tour. I've participated in fifteen or more Annual Biking twenty-five-mile Tour da Bronx. I loved all my hobbies. But roller skating changed everything. I had to reschedule or give up some of my hobbies to participate in roller skating because it became my number ONE physical activity.

Roller skating has enhanced my social interaction with so many friends, both locally and nationally. I have skated at most of the rinks in the Tristate area including the Skate Key Roller Rink which hosted the 1990 Bronx International Roller Skating Half Marathon (13.1 miles), where I participated and was awarded a first place trophy for my age bracket. I also skated at the Branch Brook Park Roller Skating Center in Newark, NJ; Central Park Skate Circle in N.Y.C.; Edward Murray Memorial Skating Center in Yonkers, NY; Wollman Rink, Central park; Riverbank State Park, N.Y.C; Brooklyn Skates in Brooklyn; Skate 22 Roller Skating Rink in Union City, NJ; Hot Skates, Lynbrook, NY; and the Pier 2 Skating Rink at Chelsea Pier, N.Y.C. Unfortunately, most of these rinks are closed. My love for the sport has taken me across the United States to Los Angeles, Venice Beach, Chula Vista, Rialto (CA), Las Vegas (NV), St Louis (MO), Virginia Beach, Richmond (VA), Detroit (MI), Chicago (IL), Atlanta (GA), Cincinnati (OH), Baltimore (MD), Charlotte (NC), Monroe (CT), Wilmington (DE), Temple Hills (MD), New Orleans (LA) and more.

I currently skate at the USA Massapequa, NY. The Central Park Skate Circle in N.Y.C is one of my favorite outdoor skating venues sponsored by the Central Park Dance Skate Association (CPDSA), where I currently serve on the Board of Directors.

Just recently, I skated at the Three Fountain Skating Rink in West Columbia, South Carolina, near my hometown of Columbia, South Carolina. When I was young, we weren't allowed to skate at the skating rinks. It was a beautiful moment for me. I felt as if I had come full circle.

Skating has broadened my international travel and I have made so many friends and have been able to connect with so many different people all over the world.

I've experienced so much and made so many memories and received several awards and accolades over the years. Some of the best of times that stand out are:

❖ While in Las Vegas, I received a second-place trophy for the best female roller skater.

❖ During one of my trips to Atlanta, I was presented with a trophy "Congratulation to Our Senior Female Skater - Atlanta Skate-A-thon 1999." There was a gentlemen engraver for hats, clothing items, etc., and he would engrave anything that you wanted. It was at this time that I first used the phrase "SK8" in our skating community, whereas others are now using it also.

❖ In 2010, I was awarded a trophy for the best skater "In the Middle" in Huntsville, Alabama.

❖ In New Orleans, our car hydroplaned during one of their torrential rainstorms, but we didn't stop. We kept going, all for the love of roller skating.

❖ I traveled by van, air or train with my dedicated "road dogs" skate friends. We laughed, sang, danced and shared our most personal conversations with one another while on our road trips.

- I met and engaged in conversations with non-skaters, explaining and displaying my passion for roller skating. Most non-skaters were of the opinion that I was referring to artistic roller skating as opposed to style skating, line dance roller skating, etc.

- Whenever I was shopping or browsing at a flea market, I would inquire about purchasing roller skating trinkets. I currently have a collection of several unique items related to roller skating.

Skating has not only impacted my life, it changed my life for the better!

Do you feel you inspire others when you skate?

I humbly appreciate the compliments from my skate family about how much I inspire them. I am an 84-year old skater. I've never hesitated to tell my age because I am proud of every breath I've taken to live this wonderful life. I hope that if I inspire anyone it is not because of my age, but the joy I have in living life to the fullest and doing what I love to do. Skating is my joy, and I hope that when I'm doing my thing on skates that it brings others joy also. Many people have approached me and said that they are returning to skating because they see me out on the floor and if I can do it, so can they. If that's what brings them joy, then I'm glad to be the inspiration to bring happiness into their life.

What would you like your legacy to be? How do you want to be remembered?

First and foremost, I have a loving family. I would like for my family to remember me as loving, caring, and completely loyal and dedicated to each and every one of them. I hope they know how much I love and appreciate all the times they were accommodating to me, just so I could skate. They realized that skating was my passion and they encouraged and supported me because it brought so much joy to my life. Secondly, I hope that I am remembered as bringing joy to the lonely hearts when I volunteer and support the senior community. Thirdly, to my skate family, I hope that I've been a positive spokesperson by asserting my views and letting others know how beneficial roller skating has been to me and the need to keep skating alive by providing facilities for roller skaters. I've given interviews for articles written in the *NY Post*, the *Daily Beast* (*NY Times*), *New York Daily News*, and *Xtremerollers News-Zine*. I participated in video interviews with Long Island 12 News and contributed to a video for the National African Skating Archive. I also made a TV appearance on the *Rachael Ray Show*.

I hope to be remembered as an original team member of Energy in the Middle (EITM) skate club, which was founded in 2003. We were the first group of roller skaters to participate in the McDonald's Annual Gospel Fest in New York City. EITM was nominated as Skaters Choice for Favorite Inner Circle Duo/Group on May 7, 2011, and Favorite Inner Circle Skate Group on May 5, 2012. For many years, EITM has participated in the Annual African American Day Parade in Harlem, NY and the New York City Dance Parade.

I feel honored to have been inducted, together with my peers, into the Adrenalin Royal Court during the 2008 Adrenalin Award Ceremony, and I was happy to participate as a "Living Legend" at The Legends Ball held in 2019 and 2021.

I hope that I have helped individuals to feel comfortable on roller skates and showed them that age is just a number. I'm very passionate about roller skating and I hope that in some small way I have been able to share the knowledge and history of roller skating and capture the hearts of adults and children of all ages to feel inspired to keep roller skating alive and well in the community. I am forever grateful for the friendships, love, respect, and appreciation my skate family has bestowed upon me. I just hope everyone knows the feeling is so mutual!

Her name is EDNA DAVOLL, an eighty-four-year-old wonder skater from Columbia, South Carolina, who currently resides in the Big Apple of New York. She's a legend...a living legend...and she exudes power, confidence, strength and humility when she steps onto the wood. She's a hula hooper, a biker, a hiker, and an exercise queen who gives the term "Energizer Bunny" new meaning. She gives...she lives... she loves fiercely and openly. She is a wonder woman with a dynamite personality and a true sense of humor. She is Edsk8ter, the super sexy senior skating sensation! Edna dedicates this article to her awesome family who has always supported her in all of her endeavors, and to the skate community who continue to keep the dream alive.

On Social Media

FACEBOOK: Edna Davoll
INSTAGRAM: Edsk8ter

I have been inspired by many skaters...

Qasim Ellis...

...aka Killa Q from New York

What is your skate style?

Rhythmic/Artistic

What is your skate setup?

Boot: Riedell 2010 Fusion - Plate: Rolline Giotto - Wheels: All American Plus

What is your favorite skate song?

"Remember the Time" by Michael Jackson

The very first time you laced up, how did you feel?

I felt overwhelmed, but excited to learn. When you can barely stand and everyone else is skating around the rink, making it look so easy, it definitely makes you anxious to want to get on that level.

What are your hidden superpowers, something crazy unique—secret power— that others don't know about you?

I've been doing martial arts since I was three years old. I have a black belt in three different styles. I would definitely say martial arts has given me an edge when it comes to understanding weight distribution, body control, and balance.

Do you feel you inspire others when you skate?

I hope so. I have been inspired by many skaters, so I could only hope that I do the same for others around me.

How has skating impacted your life?

Skating has given me a hobby that keeps me in shape and allows me to express myself freely.

What would you like your legacy to be?

I would like to be remembered as someone who came to the rink to have a good time and enjoyed teaching others how to skate.

QASIM, aka Killa Q, is a skater that you can catch flying around the rink at top speed, cutting in and out of the crowd. Skating has allowed him to have many unique experiences in life.

Qasim has performed on live television with Mariah Carey on the *Today Show*, music videos for world famous artists like Avicii, and has appeared in numerous live performances and commercials.

Qasim is a financial advisor by day and a roller skating fanatic by night! Despite all of his cool, well-timed rhythmic moves on his skates, Qasim's dance skills off of skates are so terrible that it's clear why he spends so much time in the skating rinks and not in the night clubs!

On Social Media

FACEBOOK: Qasim Ellis

INSTAGRAM: qasimellis_

YOUTUBE: Qasim Ellis

Onni Adams

...aka Oxenfree from New York

What is your skate style?

Artistic

What is your skate setup?

Riddell 220 boot Atom gold plate

What is your favorite skate song?

"Boyz" by M.I.A (house version)

The very first time you laced up, how did you feel?

Like I was flying.

What are your hidden super powers, something crazy unique—secret power—that others don't know about you?

I'm an aerialist. Lyra hoop and pole are my hidden talents.

Do you feel you inspire others when you skate?

Of course, especially women.

How has skating impacted your life?

I've been skating since I was six years old. It *IS* my life. I never truly felt like I had an outlet outside of skating.

What would you like your legacy to be?

Intrepid. A pioneer. Someone who breaks the barriers so others won't be afraid to try.

ONNI ADAMS, also known as Oxenfree, has been skating for years. That, along with being a musician, producer, aerialist, and all-around artist, she has led a plethora of civil rights organizations, performed, and created since eighteen months old.

Fun fact about Onni: American Sign Language is her first language!

On Social Media

FACEBOOK: Onni Addams

TWITTER: Onnionnioxenfree

YOUTUBE: Onni Oxenfree

Amy Gordon
NEW YORK

> *"It's a way of moving through the world that both challenges and rewards me."*

What is your skate style?

Funky Leg Salad (I learn from everyone and throw it all together with my dressing.)

What is your skate setup?

Reidell 172s w RollLine Giotto plates

What is your favorite skate song?

"Shake Your Pom Pom" by Missy Elliot

The very first time you laced up, how did you feel?

Giddy, like I knew I was stepping into my future self, but that it might hurt.

What are your hidden superpowers, something crazy unique—secret power—that others don't know about you?

I speak Dutch and have a four octaves singing range.

Do you feel you inspire others when you skate?

Yes. I see a look come over people's faces like, "I wanna do that!" And I'm a ham, so it eggs me on to do sillier, more daring moves— that way, we inspire each other.

What would you like your legacy to be?

Intrepid. A pioneer. Someone who breaks the barriers so others won't be afraid to try.

How has skating impacted your life?

It's a way of moving through the world that both challenges and rewards me. Skaters are such a cool crew, too. We're flying and bouncing and rolling around each other just happy for the vibes, learning from each other and dancing 'til we drop—sometimes literally.

What would you like your legacy to be?

A funny lady that made wrestling with one's demons look like a skate in the park.

On Social Media

FACEBOOK & INSTAGRAM:
AmyGForce

YOUTUBE:
Amy Gordon Entershamements

AMY G is a comedian, writer, actor, and singer who has played on television, films, and stages in forty-five countries around the world, won an Olivier Award with La Soiree on London's West End, and was the Big Apple Circus' first female solo comedian ever. She's building a house from the ground up with her husband in upstate New York, loves to cook, and finds comfort and joy in learning new stupid human tricks.

Her pandemic gig: recording audiobooks, lifting weights, and trying to roll a quarter on her belly like the lady on Johnny Carson.

YEAR 60 PHOTOGRAPHY
www.y60r.com
IG: @year60photog

**QUALITY!
QUICKLY!!
TRY ME!!!**

Advertisement

"You can only beat yourself maintaining your style and showmanship skills."

ANGEL VARGAS

AKA SKAYTAH—NEW YORK

What is your skate style?

My style of Rollerskating is "Rollerdance." The history of this style is from the world of dance. To begin, I come from the world of wheels. I started from the streets of the South Bronx with copper skates that came with the key. I studied dance with JoJo's Dance, Frank Hatchett, Phill Blacks and Michael Peters. What I've learned in dance I transitioned to Skating.

What is your skate setup?

Rydell 220 boot with the sure grip classic plate mounted with all American wheels

What is your favorite skate song?

There are many. "Atomic Dog," by George Clinton, "Is It In" by Jimmy Bo Horn, "The Ghetto" by Rick James. One of my favorite songs is "More Bounce to the Ounce" by Zapp and Roger, and "Bounce Rock Skate" by Von Mason.

The very first time you laced up, how did you feel?

The first time I laced up was in 1970. I was Rollerskating with copper skates with the key. I skated on the streets and did many tricks. One main trick was the helicopter spins. Thereafter I advanced to sneaker skates—blue with yellow trims and wheels. I skated at central park while performing and touring with my brother's playing basketball on a unicycle. I then landed a job at High Rollers roller rink in NYC busting tables on skates. There I met a man from the pro shop named Peter Gallo. He was a regional artistic champion skater. He looked at my feet and told me I needed to upgrade my skates. He introduced me to my first professional skates: Rydell 220 boot with the sure grip classic plate mounted with all American wheels. I felt like a pro. My mentor Dwight Toppin trained me to become a skate guard. He had a Rollerdance group I tried to join though I was too young. One night while skating I met Steven Greenburg. He asked me to visit his roller rink called the Roxy Roller Disco. A skater's paradise which I landed a job as a skate guard. History in the making.

I competed, performed, and traveled all over the globe. I auditioned for Andrew Loyd Webber's Broadway hit show, "Starlight Express." The show opened in 1986 and closed in 1989. The show then toured the US. After the show's run, I continued to travel and perform in film, television, and commercials. With all the skills and training, I then decided to give back what I have experienced to teach roller skating.

What are your hidden superpowers, something crazy unique—secret power—that others don't know about you?

My hidden super power is dedication to train hard, staying conditioned. You can only beat yourself maintaining your style and showmanship skills. You must think out of the box and bring the mix.

Do you feel you inspire others when you skate?

Yes I do. Skaters are fixated, watching me skate. They want the smooth style I skate. That's when I decided to have a class to teach the skaters how to skate properly, learning the simplest technique.

How has skating impacted your life?

Skating has had a great impact in my life, especially for fitness and health. It keeps me in good shape. A gift of opportunity that gave me the chance to see the world, competing and performing, filling the hearts of children and families with happiness. I highly recommend to anyone to purchase a pair of skates. They will enjoy rolling on wheels, becoming a part of a beautiful culture of creativity.

What would you like your legacy to be?

"For the love of Skating" I'd like my legacy to be known and remembered for the style I created Rollerdance. I respect and support all styles of skating within the culture. Remember, we are all spiritually creative. "SKAYTAH."

ANGEL VARGAS, a native New Yorker, realized at a young age that unicycling, skating, and acting were his gifts and passion. Throughout elementary school, junior high, and senior high, he participated in all of the school plays to hone his craft.

His first professional experience was to become a member of "The World Wheelers," the first professional uniball team, and demonstrated his unicycling ability on the children's television shows: *To Tell the Truth*, *Wonderama*, and *Kids are People Too*. The professional environment inspired him to pursue theatre. Soon after, Angel appeared in Jim Henson's production of *The Muppets* as a roller skater. His resulting success in working with Jim Henson and Frank Oz led to the self originated role of Rocky IV in the Tony Award winning production of "Starlight Express" at the Gershwin theatre. During his six-year run on Broadway, Angel had the privilege of working closely with composer Andrew Lloyd Webber, director Trevor Nunn, and choreographer Arlene Philips, and from these, acquired lifelong skills that would become of great importance throughout the growth of his acting career. Following "Starlight," these skills began to manifest and Angel was asked to join the touring company, which awarded him national as well as international acclaim.

Change, *See No Evil*, and *Street Knight*, to name a few. He was also granted the supporting role of Tito Jackson in the award winning ABC production *The Jacksons: An American Dream*. Following film, Angel stepped into the television scene and co-starred in the award winning, 10th anniversary special of the CBS production *Kids Killing Kids*. Other shows included *Baywatch*, *Martial Law*, *For Your Love*, and *The Burning Zone*.

However it wasn't just the experience gained from his roles in Broadway, film, and television that molded Angel into the well-trained and firmly established talent that he is today. He has also studied closely with Sylvia Leigh Showcase Theatres, and HB Studios for acting. The Broadway Dance Center and Jo Jo's Dance Factory provided him with the needed dance skills. For training in vocals, Angel worked with Phyllis Grandy. He attended the Los Angeles Film School and Recording Workshop to gain a background in television, commercial, broadcast, digital filmmaking, cinematography, and editing. All of this is what has created the much needed and diverse background for which Angel takes much pride in having acquired.

Currently, Angel resides in New York and, along with acting; he enjoys time spent with his family and friends. Since health and fitness are of importance, Angel participates regularly in Tomiki Aikido classes, enjoys rollerskating, and running. He also takes pleasure in unicycling, racquetball, stickball, flag football, baseball, and Playstation 4, just to name a few.

On Social Media

FACEBOOK:

Skaytah Instructor/Choreographer

INSTAGRAM: Skaytah2020

YOUTUBE: Skaytah2020

Roberto Lopez

CALIFORNIA

...aka Beto
"Mooncricket" Lopez

What is your skate style?

"The Art of Freestyle"

What is your skate setup?

Riedell 336 and Reactor plates, Roller Bone 101 wheels and bearings. I chose 101 hardness and 57mm for indoor and outdoors because for dancing, it doesn't matter for indoor or outdoors. But if skating around our local lake in Oakland or long rides on trails and sidewalks then I would go with softer outdoor wheels. That's the big question people ask me what wheels should they get. I tell them depends on what they want to do as I mention above that I do.

What is your favorite skate song?

I have a lot of favorites so for each style and category of music I have favorites. If it's a slow jam then I'll have a favorite that will take me into another space and my eyes closed feeling it deep. If funk when it's the right song then I feel like I'm one of those dancers from soul train and I'll go off locking. If it's classic hip-hop like Gang Star or Big Daddy Kane I'm going to skate and dance like the 90s mixed with ground moves of bboy breaking moves. New Hip-hop I don't pay attention to the names of songs and artist I just feel their basic beats and go off to them but a few I can't remember I hear only at the rinks I like because new music makes me do new moves. Certain music that mixes up and has a break in in it that you know this is the part that I'm going to do a fast or long spin to and then bam freeze. Those kinds of songs are my favorite for that example Kool and the Gang's "Summer Madness." The sound of that iconic keyboard pitch going higher and higher I'll try and hold on tight spinning faster and faster. I love anything like this in music on skates.

The very first time you laced up, how did you feel?

I remember my first skates I was 5 and they were metal skates and I just remember having fun making sparks on the side walk. At 6 I laced up for the first time and it was the feeling with music and motion that had me wanting more. Music and roller skates, I couldn't imagine skating with no music. Even when I was sponsored in my early 20s by Roces I always had my old school boombox at the skate parks playing music. I use to have a 45 foot long 10 foot high half pipe in my back yard in high school and always had music playing. When I would slide down the hand rails I was busting bboy poses and popping and body waves while sliding and grinding them. So every time I lace up it is the same feeling as when I laced up as a kid.

What are your hidden superpowers, something crazy unique—secret power—that others don't know about you?

My hidden super powers are that I remember my lucid dreams and can go in to multiple dreams and also remember my dreams as far back as the age of 4 years old. I can hit play on them and tell you all about them from then till now but it would have to be very short versions cause it's a lifetime of powerful detailed dreams to tell.

Do you feel you inspire others when you skate?

I feel it all the time and am also surprised when people tell me in person, via messages or social media comments how I inspired them. It's always a great way to make my day knowing so.

How has skating impacted your life?

Skating has saved my life in so many ways. My life growing up was not pleasant and filled with a lot of trauma. Skating has been my biggest therapy and lifesaver. I know many people find passionate things in life to help them get through a rough life. Let's just say days when my skates are broken or if I have an injury and can't skate for more than a month I can get depressed. I have lots to do to stay busy but when I can't skate, I don't think I function very well. It's a great escape from reality, even though skating is my reality but when I'm skating to good music, it is like the great escape of anything negative or troubling in life. I don't look back or think about anything else as at that moment. On my skates, I'm happy and thankful for life. The only time I can get sad on skates is when a love song comes on, making me think of someone I miss. Sometimes, I skate off the floor, zoned out and then snap out of it and try not to let a song remind me or sadden me. Instead, I'll embrace the song and go into my own world, expressing with the song smoothly, and sometimes with so much passion. I have had people come up to me in tears because they felt what I was feeling and saw me express it as my eyes were closed. What they don't know is that I hold back tears on a song if I feel it deep enough that I skated so hard and smooth to it with expression I forget where I am but end it like I was on ice in the Olympics. Not saying I'm that good but the passion I feel in my own mind is how I feel expressing my body and skate movement to a song that can really hit me hard unexpected.

What would you like your legacy to be?

I want people to remember me as a skater who was passionate about not just skating for his community. I love organizing and putting on events which I have been doing since the early 90s. I love seeing people together skating to music, I love when I have the chance to bring people together. I want people to remember my documentary, video and photography work. My other passion is filmmaking and my current roller skate documentary I hope can be archived for the history books not just for my memory but for the memory for the people I had filmed all over the world. I want their history and skate stories to be remembered, just like this book series the viewers are currently reading by Amirah Palmer.

A photographer and videographer since his mid-teens, BETO discovered his love of the art form with his 35mm Spiderman camera at the age of five. At eighteen, Beto saved for a prosumer camera and started filming special events and weddings: his career was born. Having attended Delta College and the Art Academy for motion picture studies and photography, Beto was already working on his own documentary, a project which took him all around the United States and later to international destinations. The Bboy Connection ongoing and currently Sk8-Fever roller skate documentary. Skating has been a big passion of his life since he was a child and now at forty-eight, he has never stopped. Beto skated professionally since the 90s, doing stunts on skates and roller dance for major musician artists in big stage concerts and special events with the Velocity Circus in San Francisco.

On Social Media

FACEBOOK: mooncricketfilms
INSTAGRAM: mooncricketfilms
YOUTUBE: mooncricketfilms

SHAMAR CUNNINGHAM

*aka Miraculous Spinz
from Pennsylvania*

What is your skate style?

Spinning

What is your skate setup?

Edea Skates Snyder skate plates

What is your favorite skate song?

Musiq Soulchild's "For the Night"

The very first time you laced up, how did you feel?

The very first time I laced up I was eleven years old. I can't really describe the feeling because it was and still is inexpressible. I basically lived at the rink from my youth. Whenever I had my skates on, I had no fears or worries. I was and still have the same childlike joy whenever I skate. I remember feeling like this hobby was special and wanting to never let that feeling go.

What are your hidden superpowers, something crazy unique—secret power—that others don't know about you?

I feel like everyone that puts on a pair of skates feels like they have a certain super power. I personally cannot point out one specific thing about me that makes me feel like I have a specific super power. I like to skate without fear. I like to skate without thinking. I'm a lover of music being my biggest inspiration on skates.

Do you feel you inspire others when you skate?

There is a big part of me that wants others to be inspired when they see me skate. I have learned a lot from Irvin Williams, Tex, and many others of whom inspired me when I saw them skate.

How has skating impacted your life?

Skating has impacted my life by giving me a voice on wheels that allows me to express myself. Skating is like my paintbrush that allows me to tell a story.

What would you like your legacy to be?

I'd love to be remembered as a skater who had an undeniable love for roller-skating and roller dance. I love to spin on my skates as if my life depended on it. I also have the same love and passion for deejaying.

On Social Media

FACEBOOK:
Shamar Cunningham

INSTAGRAM:
Miraculous_Spinz

YOUTUBE:
https://youtu.be/CsorVw8C5wo

SHAMAR "Miraculous Spinz" Cunningham has been skating since eleven years of age. He has been known to captivate the eyes of the blind when he skates. At every moment, Shamar likes to give thanks to those who inspired him, including the late Anthony Smith aka Terminator Tex, Irvin Williams and more. Mr. Miraculous can be found using all his talents while instructing "Great on Skates" classes, performing and more. His tag line is "If you Ain't Sweatin You Ain't Workin'." Everyone agrees that Shamar's talent is rare and flawless. Mr. Miraculous is definitely one of a kind.

Daima K. Mbele

aka Selena/Sage
from Pennsylvania

What is your skate style?

Smooth Dance Skate

What is your skate setup?

Edea Flamenco Roller Bones Elite 103

What is your favorite skate song?

"Baby I'm Scared of You" by Womack & Womack

The very first time you laced up, how did you feel?

The very first time I put on skates was when I was very young, maybe ten or eleven years old. However, I caught the fever in my early thirties!

What are your hidden superpowers, something crazy unique—secret power—that others don't know about you?

Most people do not know that I am a school counselor and school principal. I also ride motorcycles and a former rapper and spoken word performer.

Do you feel you inspire others when you skate?

I feel that I inspire those that think they cannot skate well or are having challenges. I am a great cheerleader and encourage everyone to keep trying and embrace their own style. I continue to go to skate lessons because I did not build on good foundational skills.

How has skating impacted your life?

In my early thirties, I was newly divorced with a toddler, changing careers and had experienced a terrible loss in my family. Skating saved my sanity and my life! Skating gave me time from day-to-day struggles to gain a better perspective!

What would you like your legacy to be?

That I encouraged new skaters to keep skating and to embrace their own style!

On Social Media

FACEBOOK: Selene Keaveney

INSTAGRAM: sageskate1

SELENA, a newly divorced mom, was taking her three-year-old son to the barbershop. She told her son to just sit in any chair, because "We have other things to do today!" Little did she know that she was breaking the "barbershop rule." Her son's barber and avid skater asked Selena religiously to come skating whenever she brought her son to get his hair cut. "Skating!" Selena silently chuckled. "Skating is for kids. I am a whole adult!" But once she unknowingly broke the barbershop rule by telling her son to go to any barber, her barber (the skating barber) called and said that she had to go skating to make things right! Selena reluctantly obliged.

When she walked through the door of Franklinville (now Sk847), she heard the music, saw the lights and although she does not smoke, she could not overlook the hint of marijuana in the distance. Adults were smiling, skating, and enjoying the vibes! She greeted the skating barber, who looked at her as if to say "See? I told you!" Then she saw him! A skater that was about 300+ pounds and looked like a refrigerator gliding on wheels! It was then that she said to herself, "If he can do it, I can certainly try!" From that day to this, she has had the fever to skate and to learn!

As a school counselor and principal, Selena plans roller skating trips as incentives. She knows that skating kept her husband, King James, off the streets of North Philadelphia and has been a place of solace, peace, and joy for them both, singularly and as a couple!

James Burtin

aka King James from Philly

What is your skate style?

Freestyle Dance

What is your skate setup?

Edea Fly on Sure Grips

What is your favorite skate song?

Dance House Song

The very first time you laced up, how did you feel?

I was about five or six years old and I was excited!

What are your hidden superpowers, something crazy unique—secret power—that others don't know about you?

I am able to fix just about anything! There is strength in my quietness. Some call me the quiet storm.

Do you feel you inspire others when you skate?

Yes, I feel like I help others to visualize their own capacity.

How has skating impacted your life?

Growing up in North Philadelphia, skating gave me hours of enjoyable fun and activity. It kept me grounded and out of the streets. I felt that I could accomplish things that others had little knowledge about.

What would you like your legacy to be?

I want to be remembered as a TRUE skater!

"James, Raheem, and Kisha! Y'all have to get out the house today!" James' mother exclaimed. Asia, a mother of three was tired of the kids getting on her nerves so she took them to the skating rink! James was nine years old and the oldest. He put on the brown skates with the big orange wheels and was ready! The first time on the floor was an adventure! James realized that his body could do things on wheels that he simply could not do just by walking. And suddenly, he could go FAST, REALLY FAST! Skating became a major obsession and a foundation in the life of James. James has appeared in two HBO presentations and draws crowds every time he is on the floor. Secretly, James is a comedian who does great impersonations of friends and family members! James could be a great skate instructor if he stayed still long enough. Catch him if you can!

James met his wife, Selena, at the skating rink. They enjoy skating date nights as a couple and travel extensively to skate!

INSTAGRAM: king.james522

Mataji Armour Bey

aka Lady M from New York

What is your skate style?

Rink and dance

What is your skate setup?

220 Douglass Snyder

What is your favorite skate song?

"Kitale" by Sam One

The very first time you laced up, how did you feel?

I felt very excited and nervous to execute and master the art of skating.

What are your hidden superpowers, something crazy unique—secret power—that others don't know about you?

Remote viewing.

Do you feel you inspire others when you skate?

Yes, I do feel like I inspire others, whether it's with the fashion I'm wearing or the combination of my skate dance moves that put smiles on people's faces and makes them want to get on their skates.

How has skating impacted your life?

Skating has impacted my life by giving me more opportunities to showcase my abilities in the acting and entertainment industries. I'm proud to be a part of skate legends, aka Smooth Edges where I can look back and say, "Yes! That's my peoples." (LOL)

What would you like your legacy to be?

I would like my legacy to be the sweet sassy actor, fashionista, chef, and multi-talented young lady. I want to be remembered as the sweetheart, a well spoken young woman who never gave up and always persevered, who kept going by, dabbing in different activities and travels.

MATAJI ARMOUR BEY, born and raised in Brooklyn, New York, grew up in a loving, supportive, and business-oriented home. She began her journey with entrepreneurship with skin care products to jewelry and clothing. Despite Mataji's different business ventures, she found her next niche of face painting for various events and parties throughout the Tri-state. With eighteen years of creativity, Mataji wanted to showcase her talents so she began modeling, and years later, she fell in love with acting in theater and film. Taking on different roles, Mataji never looked back. Along with Mataji's favorite hobby, horseback riding, her favorite food is Italian. She says, "I will never eat a fake noodle 'cause that's an impasta."

On Social Media

FACEBOOK: Empresslove Bey

INSTAGRAM: Mataji_ladym

YOUTUBE: Empress lady M

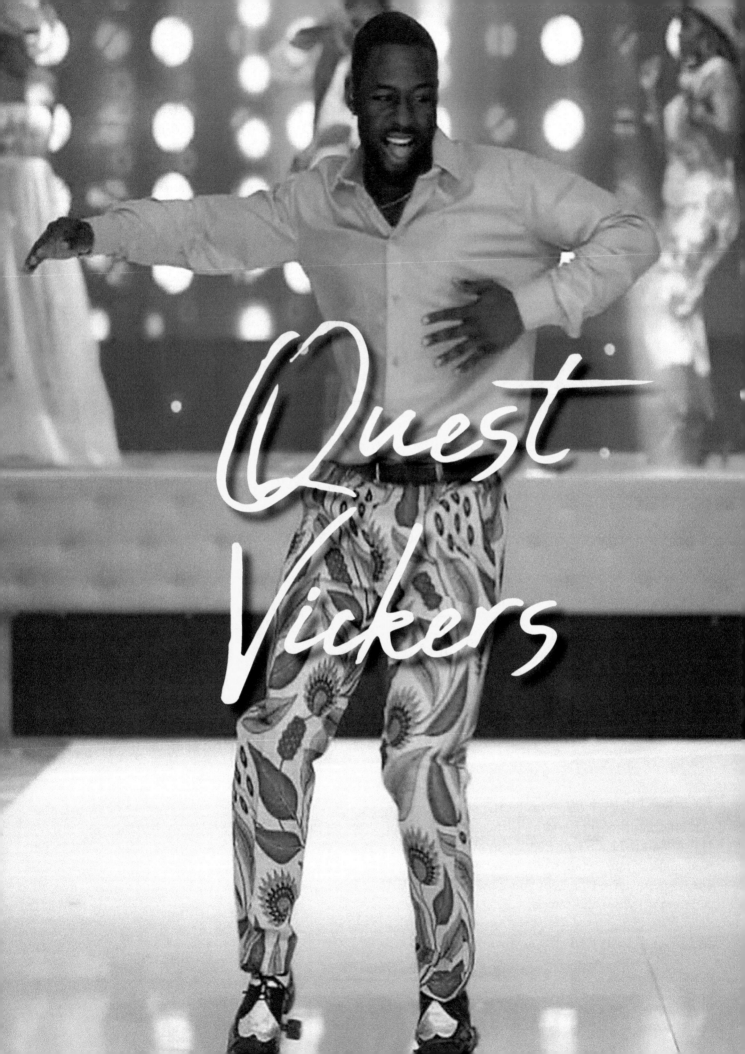

...aka Quest Love from California

What is your skate style?

LA Freestyle—its a cultural state style that allows you to express yourself with everything you feel. It is important to implement the tradition, originality, and history of Los Angeles in your skating.

What is your skate setup?

Stacey Adams Dress shoe with a sure-grip plate.

What is your favorite skate song?

LBC Crew's "Best Beware of My Crew." That's a West Coast rap song that I find my joy when skating. The beat of that song gets me going to entertain.

The very first time you laced up, how did you feel?

My first time skating was in 2007. I was invited to a birthday party and the reason why I started skating was because I was inspired by what I saw other skaters doing. Just being in the skating rink felt like home, like I belonged there. As I continued to attend skating, my motivation increased. Being motived by older skaters really took my attention and focus and I began to train myself mentally and physically to be good and I continued to practice until I got better.

What are your hidden superpowers, something crazy unique—secret power—that others don't know about you?

Faith is my superpower. Faith has opened doors for me that no man could have opened. Faith is believing without conformation.

Do you feel you inspire others when you skate?

I do feel that I inspire others when I skate. Skating to me is living. I skate week in and week out. I take skating personal because it is what I love to do. I put all of my time and love in perfecting my craft. No one can take the skate love that I have inside of me away. I am real and true to the skate culture. I am true to my roots. Skating is what I love to do and it makes me happy each and every time I lace up.

How has skating impacted your life?

Skating has impacted my life by providing opportunities to appear in music videos with great artists such as The Migos/Drake "Walk It Talk It," Black Eyed Peas, Snoop Dogg "Be Nice," and Terry and Rebecca Crews "Reaching." I appeared in a Buzzfeed documentary about other skaters and a Bese documentary for Zoe Saldana and a TV appearance on *Little Women LA*.

What would you like your legacy to be?

I want my legacy to be that I have always given 100% every time I skate. I want to be remembered as a skater who cared about the skate culture and who cared about others. I want people to know that my heart for skating is full of love. I found love and passion in skating and love and passion helped me care about the skate legacy.

On Social Media

FACEBOOK: questlovetoskat

INSTAGRAM: questlove_

QUEST VICKERS is a California nativ
and lifelong skater. He goes by the name o
Quest Love. He is a sponsored skater by Floy
Mayweather and he travels nationally doing wha
he loves, roller skating. He has appeared in musi
videos and documentaries and has also hosted hi
own skate event in 2021—Quest Love Skate Jan
The world is his oyster.

Advertisement

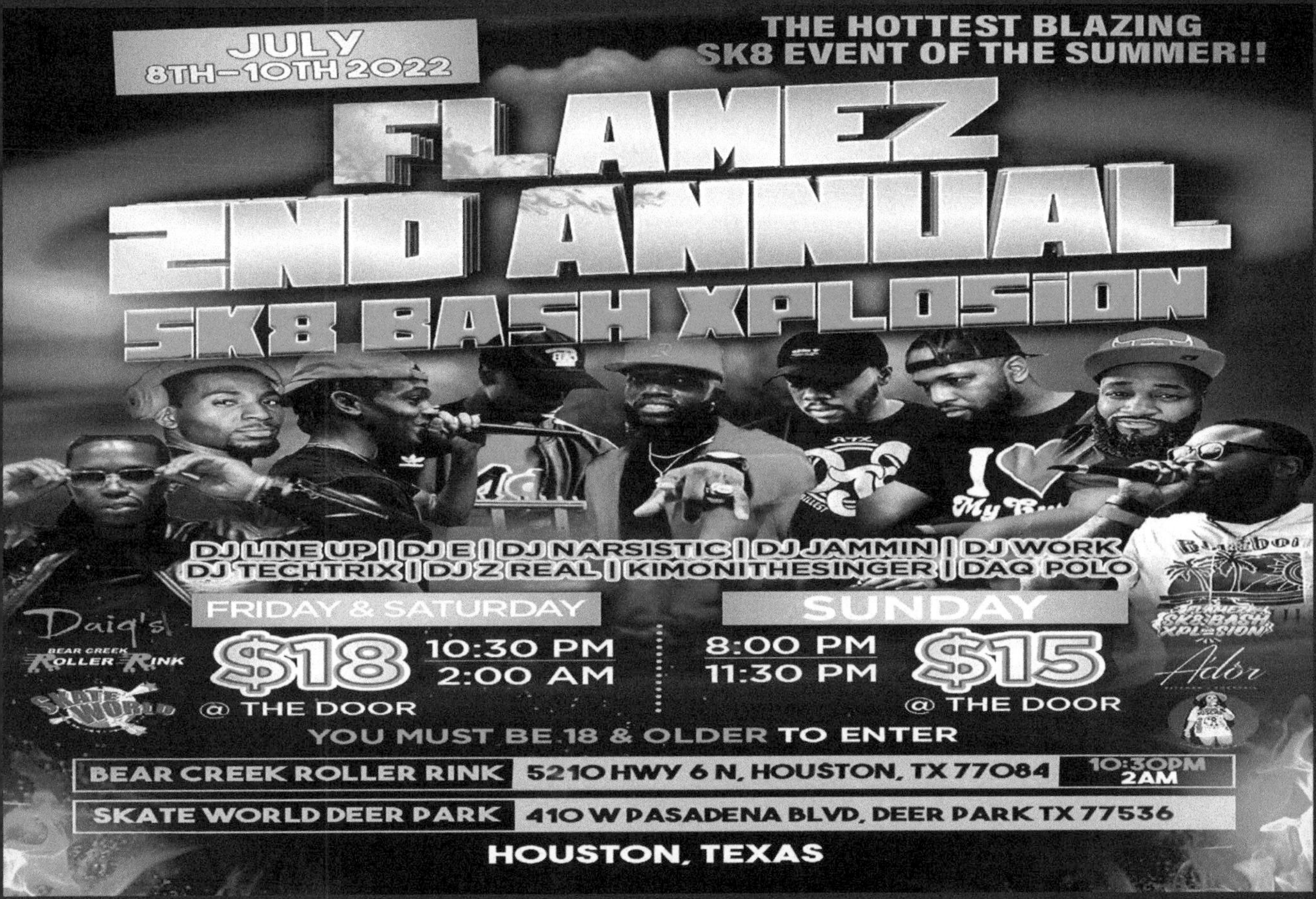

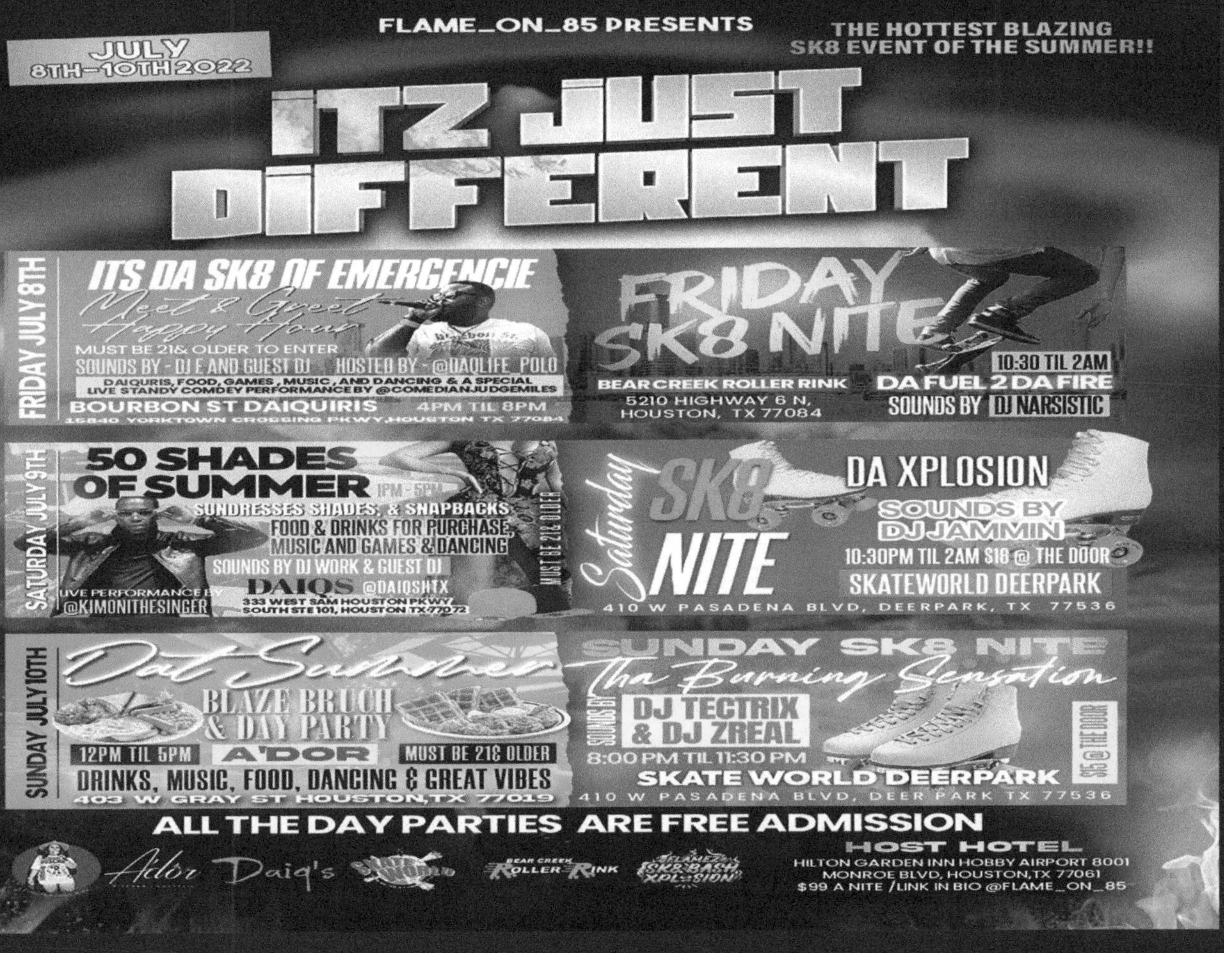

Jillian Burgess

aka Jill_tf_out from New York

What is your skate style?

Freestyle

What is your skate setup?

Riedell 3200/ Roll-line Giotto plate/ Chicago vanathane wheels

What is your favorite skate song?

"Gonna Make You Sweat" by C&C Music Factory

The very first time you laced up, how did you feel?

The first time I ever put skates on, I was so little, my mom put these plastic ones from Toys R Us on my feet and I'd shuffle around the apartment, screaming, "Mommy, look I'm skating!" The excitement had not changed. After thirteen years of casual skating, I bought my own pair of roller skates in 2018 and you guessed it, I was showing my mother how effortlessly I could destroy her wood floors. I felt jubilant, liberated and eager to learn how to dance in them, the first time I laced up again.

What are your hidden superpowers, something crazy unique—secret power—that others don't know about you?

No crazy superpowers! But I'm a fast learner, and my eagerness and ability to show others how to do things had many people question why I don't teach professionally. Honestly, I just have more fun being the student. Teachers are literally everywhere. Sometimes they find you.

Do you feel you inspire others when you skate?

Yes, only because it's a never ending song I hear from new skaters and people who watch me enjoy my life on wheels. Everyone wants to feel good mentally and physically, so they inquire about it! What makes it even more rewarding is when you see the people you gave pointers to evolve and groove in their own way.

How has skating impacted your life?

Skating is a cult, and the moment you have a good time on them it's like the community encourages and inspires you to come back. When I started attending skaterobics classes in 2019, Ms. Tanya Dean made it known that when we come in to skate, we leave all that craziness, anger, bad day nonsense, any problems at the door, and that's exactly what I have been doing every chance I skate. It helped me process a lot of repressed emotions and irrational fears. Depression hasn't been much of a problem because skating has kept my mood up. I've become more confident in my abilities, and became more motivated to set goals for myself, both life and skill wise. Skating is medicine when done safely and thanks to it, I've been off antidepressants for three years now.

What would you like your legacy to be?

I'd like to be remembered for my energy I put out into encouraging others to see their potential. Not everyone has someone rooting for them and seeing those individuals who are now taking charge in not only skating but in life in general warms my soul and in return encourages me to continue my journey.

On Social Media?

INSTAGRAM: Jill_TF_Out

Her name is JILLIAN BURGESS, but she prefers to be addressed as Jill. She is a genuine, kind-hearted soul to all and her freestyle approach to dancing on skates inspires others to give it try. Her skate journey is in the beginning stages. She participated in a roller-skate fashion show this past summer, and is now helping other beginner skaters learn routines that will build up their confidence and muscle memory to execute skate moves they see many other seasoned skaters do. She enjoys making others feel comfortable and happy. Many people she comes across are surprised to find out she's also a school nurse. Then the welcoming aura, the silly rhymes/phrases she blurts out while breaking down skate moves will begin to make sense.

Rochelle Pollard

From New York

What is your skate style?

Freestyle

What is your skate setup?

Reidell 3200 Giotto Plante, Original Roller Bone Wheels, Fafnir bearings

What is your favorite skate song?

"Don't Waste My Time" by Usher/Ella Mae

The very first time you laced up, how did you feel?

I started my journey in the world of roller-skating when I was about six or seven, with my metal skates. I sometimes skated with other children, but most often I rolled solo. Music was not a factor with street skating as a child. We just went outside and enjoyed the simplicity of feeling free, moving, and enjoying the peace and fun that it brought in the moment. As I look back, that is what I describe it to be, but then… it was simply "FUN." Generations now often wonder how we did things in such a manner. I would often hear younger skaters say, "How did you do that? Skate for hours, and no music, and actually enjoy it?" I think then, it was about being able to get out of the house as a kid. We did not have the technologies we see now, so we had to be ever so creative to fill our time. It was my opportunity to feel unrestricted. I rolled around for hours on the weekend in my neighborhood. Why was it so fascinating to roll at that time? I cannot explain it, but that was the life then. Life was great on skates as a kid. Eventually, I would transition to skating rinks somewhere at around age ten or so. My parents and other family would meet up at a rink on Long Island called Walcliff Rink with a dry wood floor, rails, and organ music. Laughing for hours with my family; it was the best time in my life. Then came life at age sixteen. When I stepped into the rinks then, it was a completely different vibe. I would soon get lost in the beats.

The eighties and nineties as a roller skater had to be the absolute best time in life. The best music, great skaters. I would soon become addicted to the life and skated every chance I got. It was a source of fun, but also my escape from a trouble household. The one person who afforded me an education and a pair of Reidell 220s with a quick graduation to a 192 boot was both good and not so good. Roller skating created a balance in life and would become what I see it to be today. A way of life and an activity that would bring not just fun, but peace and balance.

What are your hidden superpowers, something crazy unique—secret power—that others don't know about you?

I don't really have hidden super powers, but what I will say, I have a way with words when telling the story and having the ability to enhance it in a matter of moments. I wouldn't say it's a secret, though.

Do you feel you inspire others when you skate?

When I hear the word *phenomenal*, what does that mean, really? It's when skaters say things like "Thank you, Chelle. I recognize what you do in the skate community and the passion you have for roller skating and for the skate community." "Just the thought and action to make something happen for those who live more on the upper parts of our beautiful island. We greatly appreciate what you do." It is rewarding to hear skaters share their testimonies about how appreciative they are about my role and actions within the skate community. Growing up in my home, I never received any validation or recognition, so there are many instances when it is given to me in my adult life, it is difficult to process when someone shares their appreciation for how I engage the skate community, when I am supportive of a skater/skater advocate. In the beginning, I never accepted accolades and at times, I am only just now beginning to accept when skaters speak positive toward me.

The testimonies of others is my validation that I am doing something positive in the Skate World Community and it is not only fulfilling, but rewarding. To know that my actions create positive experiences for others in the community, is a "Mission Accomplished" moment.

How has skating impacted your life?

Roller Skating has kept me emotionally balanced. It has provided me with the ability to take control of my wellness journey, both physically and mentally. It has been a grounder for me and has great therapeutic value in my life.

As a child, I enjoyed my home space, but I had so much more fun when I was outdoors. Wollman Rink had that feel like the TV Show Episode of the Honeymooners. Old-fashioned rink, with that dry wood floor, rails, and organ music. My cousins and I rolled around the outer part of the rink, holding the rails and, of course, falling and laughing at ourselves. We also laughed at the seasoned skaters that were in the middle working on their edges, circle patterns, and turns/pivots. Some were wearing dance attire that to us kids "looked funny" so of course with that came laughter. I do not want to labor a conversation on my life as a child growing up with metal skates or even the stories to be told of life in the rink in my adolescent years. That was all great fun. As the years moved, so did life, and when the age of disco skating came the 220-dance boot and the Douglas Snyder deluxe dance plate. Those boots lasted about 4 to 6 months before I complained that they literally "sucked." Not because they were not comfortable. They were white boots and stayed messy with all the falls I took as I was learning how to disco roller-skate. Boot covers

were a joke, so I asked my dad to buy me a pair of black boots. The cool part, not only did I get the black boot, but I was also able to upgrade to a 192 boot, which, I still have and from time to time, still skate in them. They are a bit snug after my second child. OMG, my foot grew a half inch. Still skate-friendly, but with thin socks.

Many people will tell you that roller skating is a form of therapy. My Therapeutic Zones were Skate World in Queens and Laces in New Hyde. These places are long gone as is my alternate favorite spot, Hot Skates. When I found my way back into the Skate World, I vowed I would never, ever mistreat my eights again. Understandably, there was a time I had to take a back seat due to a skate-related injury I sustained at the new KEY. I was coming back strong; I was in my late thirties and still feeling my best. It was a bad night because one of the skaters was quite reckless. I was going into a right outside pivot and as I was completing this, a skater barreled into me and sent me in the opposite direction of my turn. Problem with that, I was already into the turn, and my weight sent me turning in the opposite direction while in the turn. I went down and my friends were yelling at me to get up. Yeah, the dude had to weigh at least 250 pounds. As I tried to get up, I could not do anything with my right leg. Finally, a floor guard helped me off the floor. I packed up and hobbled out to my Green Aerostar that looked like a Scooby Doo Truck. I could not bend my right leg. What a mess, and I could not leave my truck in the neighborhood, because I still had Detroit plates on the truck. OMG. So, being clever I put the truck in low gear and drove home with my left foot. The ish you do when you skate.

What would you like your legacy to be?

I would like to be remembered as a skater that took the time to see those who were not seen, not having big voices, and being supportive, advocating for changes within the skate community that would keep skaters with the ability to roll and stay fit, youth to be able to roll on wheels and learn the values of networking, social skills, and having a fun way to stay fit. I would also desire to be one that was instrumental in effecting positive change within the skate world community. Rather we lose rinks, creating a platform of advocacy for the community to win and not lose rinks.

CHELLE aka Lady Flightroller is an awesome person and never thinks of herself. She is always looking out for the next person. As a skater, she has always brought people together. In her early skate life, she worked closely with her father to create a dance group in the early 1980s. The dance group comprised skate youth from the community and together they created dance routines and put on shows at Skate World In Queens. Chelle was well-liked by the skaters, like a big sister. So you see, much like how she operates now, she has always been one to just pick up and do for others, selflessly. Chelle's current drive focuses on acquiring spaces for skaters to skate, given that New York is no longer a thriving Skate City. Since the pandemic, Chelle has mobilized within the Skate World Community and has been pressing forward to locate/secure skate spaces for the community. Chelle understands the importance and the value of creating this for the community. Health and wellness are important to her, since she lost both parents to major health issues, and also issues that would create disruptions with emotional wellness for her mother. Domestic issues, health issues, etc were some things Chelle would see in her immediate household and she would tell you, "Roller skating saved my life."

As we move about in the Skate World as we know it now, we all witness the documentary where it illustrated Skating Rinks Across America and the major impact felt by all, when we systematically lost rink after rink. New York was one of those cities that had a vibrant skate community and rinks to entertain all. But as quickly as we saw the rise, we saw the fall. When we lost yet another mainstay rink out in Lynbrook, New York, Hot Skates, it set Chelle's wheels in motion to find skate parties and bring skaters together. She knew there was a Community of Skaters beyond New York, and she was determined to link, network, and promote the experiences across the map. With this, Skate Info Network formed, not knowing that it would evolve to what we see today. Skate Info Network is going on its third year, with skater links in various states that act as anchors in their region where skaters can connect. Not everyone in the community will see the value of the Network, and some do. Again, the original vision was finding parties. Established on April 18, 2019, the Network has grown and the roles of those who were and continue to be involved have supported the new and improved version of the Network. It is an LLC Platform that focuses on support, troubleshooting, promoting, hosting, and advocacy.

It seemed like yesterday, Chelle would get calls from skaters who were hosting skate parties and was getting a lot of positive feedback for creating the group and how it was moving as far as content. The advice at that time was "Don't change what you are doing with the group, let it grow into what it will become." Fast forward, here we are today, and Chelle is now the curator of a growing online National Social Media Skate Platform that is recognized in 26 states and 39 countries and well respected. The platform has continued to exist and be not only present but relevant. The first stages were devoted to finding skate groups online and reaching out to see what skaters were up to, and what could be done to jump-start these groups to find new energy and to let others know of their existence. Sounds foolish enough and some folks said, "Why bother?" Chelle just said, "Why not?!" These groups dated back to 2014/2015 and with no activity. Today, the group's presence on social media has exploded. And while we were in a movement before the pandemic, we are very much alive, present, and relevant. We can partially attribute some of it to our new life post the pandemic and the dawn of TikTok. One of the goals was to look for skaters who had a presence at one point in time. Chelle vowed she would do her part to contribute to the growth and integrity of the skate community and that we would not be the face of "irrelevant." She would put effort into this mission. "Keeping Roller Skating Alive." Especially, since so many skaters say they find skating therapeutic and fun. Phenomenal Skater she is. Why? Because she is here, present, and with a mission to support the next wave of skaters. A skater who wears a Skate Advocacy Hat proudly, and willingly goes the distance to support others, troubleshooting situations where necessary. Always with a smile, and when faced with adversity, she still presses forward. The naysayers, backstabbing, crab in the barrel dwellers are merely the fuel that moves her to continue to roll. What's the expression going around these days? She understands the "Assignment." Again, this is not for everyone out here, and it is understood, unconventional ways are not always received by all, and that's okay. When you find yourself moving in ways that seemingly have been designed for you, and you recognize it and accept it, not much else matters. When you hear, or receive a message from a skater that says, "Thank you for taking the time to find ways for us to continue to enjoy skating, especially when the weather changes and we can't be in the park," speaks volumes.

With the creation of the platform, a few key things have happened, all to benefit skaters. Skate Info Network collaborated in October 2019 with the first Bronx CommUNITY Skate. It was awesome, but then came the pandemic that slowed the world. As we slowly emerge from pandemic mode, the Network has created a partnership with the Sk8Family out of West Columbia, South Carolina, and had two extremely successful events. It was told that it could not be done, but it happened, it was successful and skaters had fun. We also had a successful summer and created a skating experience from Bronx Skaters in the park and it was totally awesome. And the beauty of it all, Skate Info Network gets to run that back in 2022. Oh, and there is one other success to mention. Now that the brand is fully licensed, there are some pretty cool skate products online, including that wonderful "Skater's Pledge" T-shirt that was created right after the loss of Hot Skates. We strive to keep Roller Skating Alive, and we are here to uplift the Skate Community and preserve/protect the Culture. Roller skating has always been, it is nothing new. What do those numbers look like in a Pandemic World? Not sure, but skaters are plentiful for sure. We know that because skates are backlogged for months on end, I will close this with a "Stay Tuned to Skate Info Network, that Powerhouse Online Skate Platform" "You know… the one we always say, "Where it's a S.I.N. not to know!!! Phenomenal Skater, Chelle. Always looking for ways to enhance, support, improve and bring a few hours of fun, relaxation and joy. For the Love of Skating.

On Social Media

FACEBOOK GROUP:
Skate Network Info, LLC

INSTAGRAM:
skateinfonetwork

YOUTUBE:
Rochelle Pollard

Natasha Thurman
aka Skate Beast,
Illinois

What is your skate style?

Rhythm Acrobatic and performer Style

What is your skate setup?

Riedell 120 boots, with Flo Max and Jam Wheels. I mix them to accommodate the different stunts and floors/stages on which I perform.

What is your favorite skate song?

I don't have a specific favorite. I love anything that has deep bass and moves my soul. Songs that make me want to dance and zone out like no one is there but me.

The very first time you laced up, how did you feel?

The very first time I laced up I felt excitement and joy. I felt freedom and melodic.

What are your hidden superpowers, something crazy unique—secret power—that others don't know about you?

When its time to perform, my adren-alin turns into pure energy and I turn into "Tashae'." That is the dancer side of me. I infused that with Skate Beast and I simply zone out. The performer side is activated and there's no filter. I see no one except that camera and those lights. Its my time and I shine. I let nothing negative in and I let God take over.

Do you feel you inspire others when you skate?

Yes, people always reach out to let me know the impact I have had on them. How they have become more confident in their own style and are not worried about what others think. They simply enjoy how I move in positivity and confidence. They say they are inspired by how I move with athleticism, but still maintain my femininity in how I roll. The ladies especially say how they want to feel and skate sexy, yet classy. They like that I have that balance and that inspires them to do the same. To not be scared to try new things.

How has skating impacted your life?

Skating has had an incredible impact on my life because I feel free and creative on my wheels. It has changed the way I view the world. It has given me a greater outlook on how skating can affect millions of lives in a positive way. It has impacted my health, keeping me fit, bringing me happiness and excitement. It has brought financial increase, spiritual strength, travel adventures and blessed friendships. My practice sessions are more rewarding and it has impacted the success of my team: Glide8orz. It gave me a determination to never give up. It is not just a recreation for me, but a way of life, a business venture... a heartbeat. That's why, for me, it will always be my Sk8 luv.

What would you like your legacy to be?

I want to simply be remembered the way I know God would want me to be, that I put Him first, that before all the open doors, the opportunities, increase, wonderful relationships I developed. If it wasn't for His grace, His hand on my life, nothing would have happened. I told him I would give Him all the glory, and as a result, He gave it all to me. I want people to remember the encouraging conversations we had. The private prayer sessions, the big warm hugs and laughs we had. That I was always about team and working together. That I was always about positivity and good energy. That I was about confidence and a firm believer in being yourself, knowing your God-given purpose. That I pushed against arrogance and pride, and promoted humility. That I never gave up on my skate dreams. I was resilient and very determined to get the job done. No matter how it may have looked, I stayed hopeful of the future being bright.

Natasha Thurman's Achievements

- Nike Skate Ad and Model (Made History)
- Award winning United Skates Documentary character/skate feature
- 7 trophies and more including 3 Adrenalin Skate Awards with Josh Smith "Batsmoke" my skate partner
- America's Got Talent Contestant with Glide8orz crew
- Winning Several money prizes
- Being a Skate Judge for several Competitions
- Helping Host Skate parties and for entertainment
- Meeting Celebrities
- Won a trip to London to perform with international DJ Moodymann on an Island in front of millions of people...I crowd surfed
- Performing for Universoul Circus and Aloft Circus
- Did several TV appearances like WGN, ABC, Windy City Live, Steve Harvey Show, The CHI, Empire TV show
- I've done Music videos, Instructional videos, team workshops
- Performed for special celebrations like weddings/birthdays/graduations

Tidbits/funny facts about Natasha

- I'm a Christian/faith Believer
- I'm a professional dancer who loves to sing and perform
- Grew up in a performing Arts Family
- I'm a animal lover
- I'm a night bird so please don't expect a response at 6/7am in the morning cuz I'm sleep
- I do not like spiders
- I'm a multitasker
- I'm a sports fan
- I'm a super hero and marvel fan
- I'm adventurous and fun
- I'm like sugar but I got a kick like spice so never underestimate me, I'm a quiet storm
- I love amusement parks and water
- I went sky diving and loved it

On Social Media?

INSTAGRAM:

skatebeastbeautyn

Sophia Dawson

New York

What is your skate style?

Rhythm Acrobatic and performer Style

What is your skate setup?

Riedell Boot and plates with All American Wheels

What is your favorite skate song?

I found a place (Where we can boogie)

The very first time you laced up, how did you feel?

The first time I laced up I was about seven or eight years old. We were in Toys R Us and my parents were buying me my first pair of skates. It was a moment of instant joy.

What are your hidden superpowers, something crazy unique—secret power—that others don't know about you?

I carry the spirit of God, which allows me to do the same things that Jesus did.

Do you feel you inspire others when you skate?

I feel more like I am inspired by others when I skate. I am not sure if I am an inspiration. I love watching aging individuals skate and seeing that they are able to do things that my body has not yet learned. I love when they are speeding past me during their favorite house song and I find myself barely being able to keep up or catch my breath. I am inspired by those who are beginners one day and then teachers the next. I think that my life outside of the skate floor inspires others. So when I show up on the skate floor they are excited to know that I am still a part of this community, regardless of where life takes us.

How has skating impacted your life?

Skating has been a safe space and it used to be my secret place. I am convinced that God used skating to keep me out of trouble during my teenage years and to keep me happy and joyous during the years that are often challenging as I switched from being a child to becoming an adult. It was where I first learned what community felt like. To this day, skating still brings me much joy.

What would you like your legacy to be?

I want to be remembered as a woman of God, who brought the kingdom wherever she went, even onto the skate floor.

On Social Media?

FACEBOOK:

sophiadawson90

INSTAGRAM:

iamwetpaint

SOPHIA DAWSON, 33, is a Brooklyn and Atlanta based visual artist who has dedicated her life's work to exposing the stories and experiences of individuals who are striving to overcome the injustices they face both individually and collectively. By raising awareness of these individuals she aims to humanize social justice issues and to prevent such experiences from being repeated in the future. Some of the individuals featured in her work include mothers who have lost their children to police brutality both past and present, the Exonerated 5 and political prisoners from the Black Liberation movement that are still incarcerated within the United States.

Sophia holds a bachelor's degree in fine arts from the School of Visual Arts and a masters degree in visual arts administration from New York University. Her work has recently been exhibited in Rush Arts Gallery and the Bronx Museum for the Arts as well as the 2020 US Open. She is a recent participant of the Whitney Museum's Independent Study program and a recent resident of the Bronx Museum of Art's first residency program. She is a 2020 PAIR Artist fellow working with the Mayor's Office of Criminal Justice. She facilitates art workshops at Rikers Island through her company I Am Wet Paint and also became a member of the faculty of the Fine Art Department at the School of Visual Arts in 2020. In 2020, Sophia was one of three artists selected to design the "Black Lives Matter" street mural for Foley Square in New York City. Throughout the spring and summer of 2020 her public art for the movement was featured in Forbes Magazine, on New York 1 and on ABC Nightline.

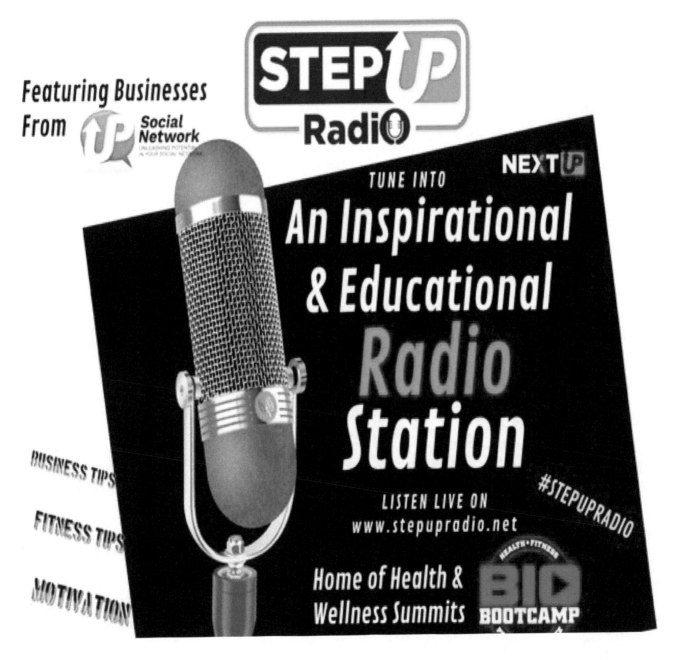

ROGER GREEN
aka Roger G, New York

"I can motivate anyone and bring the best out of them."

What is your skate style?

Pop lock and break

What is your skate setup?

Freestyle

What is your favorite skate song?

"Bounce, Rock, Skate, Roll"

The very first time you laced up, how did you feel?

I felt like a king.

What are your hidden superpowers, something crazy unique—secret power—that others don't know about you?

I can motivate anyone and bring the best out of them.

Do you feel you inspire others when you skate?

Yes, I inspire anyone who watches me.

How has skating impacted your life?

It made me want to help others because of my talent.

What would you like your legacy to be?

I want to be remembered as one of the best skaters who has ever done it.

ROGER G. is known as The G Man when he is on skates. He appeared in movies and videos like Michael Jackson's "Who's Bad" in the 1980s. He even sported a jeri curl back then and if you walked behind him too closely, you might have slipped and fallen.

On Social Media

FACEBOOK: ROGER GREEN

INSTAGRAM: ROGERG4LIFE

YOUTUBE: ROGERG

Ishmael Alvarado
New York

ISHMAEL ALVARADO grew up in the Lower East Side of Manhattan, he had dreams of being a performer/artist through Roller Skating and Break Dancing as well as through Martial Arts. So to pursue those dreams at the age of 17 he enlisted in the Marines where they let him express his artistic talents. After serving his country for 8 years he came back home to New York City and found a career as a Sales Executive for a National Distributor of Janitorial Supplies and Equipment. Adulting, as they call it today, came with financial security for him, but his childhood dreams of becoming a performer were still deeply rooted inside of him. He then went back to his old Karate School (DAS Karate Federation) and earned his Black Belt from Martial Arts Hall of Fame Instructor Master Nathan Ingram. He also brushed the dust off his Quad Roller Skates and got back his groove at Roxy Roller Rink, Central Park Skate Circle and actively a member of the Rollerwave Skate Family. He's currently proud father of two amazing kids, A Self Defense Instructor and active DAV local chapter member where he advocates for Veterans' rights.

What is your skate style?

Roxy Skate Style

What is your skate setup?

Original Riedell Silver Star Boots (1983) Douglas Snyder Plates and All American Plus Wheels

What is your favorite skate song?

"Blame it on the Boogie," by Michael Jackson

The very first time you laced up, how did you feel?

When I was 12 years old I started skating in the "Disco Roller Skating" era and my first time at Roxys was breathtaking and I knew I had fallen in love with dancing on roller skates!

What are your hidden superpowers, something crazy unique—secret power—that others don't know about you?

I'm a 5th Degree Karate Black Belt

Do you feel you inspire others when you skate?

Yes! I give and feed energy when I dance on skates!

How has skating impacted your life?

It made me want to help others because of my talent.

What would you like your legacy to be?

I want to be known as a good dad to my kids, an amazing Martial Artist, a United States Marine and one of the greatest roller skaters in New York City.

On Social Media?

FACEBOOK: Ishmael Alvarado

INSTAGRAM: Shihan2013

YOUTUBE: Ishmael Alvarado

What is your skate style?

Rhythm, Freestyle, Samba

What is your skate setup?

Riedell OG 172, Imperial Snyder plates, All American Plus wheels

What is your favorite skate song?

"Gypsy Woman" by Crystal Waters

The very first time you laced up, how did you feel?

My first pair of skates were the metal kind when I was seven. I may have been eleven or twelve, when I officially laced up in a proper roller rink. It was the most exciting and impatient feeling ever, trying to get my skates on as fast as possible!

What are your hidden superpowers, something crazy unique—secret power—that others don't know about you?

My superpower is empathy and intuition.

Do you feel you inspire others when you skate?

Yes, I do. Pretty often, new sk8ers will roll up to me and tell me how much they enjoyed my skating style and would love to sk8 like me. I've had people just come and dance with me and do the stuff that I'm doing or try to. My experience is that, we sk8ers inspire and encourage one another, it happens naturally.

How has skating impacted your life?

For me, sk8ing is a musical, spiritual, emotional and physical outlet. Using sk8ing as a meditation, and a way to clear my head or work out challenges has definitely made me healthier and happier. It's absolutely helped me with my mental outlook.

What would you like your legacy to be?

That I gave my all and did my best.

Holistic therapist, percussionist, artist and rollerskater, NANCY VALDES was born in Spanish Harlem and raised in the Soundview section of the Bronx. She sk8ed early, at age 7, but hated the metal skates because they vibrated too much. By age 11, her mom started taking her to a few of the rinks that were in the Bronx, Rollerena and Skate Key and Stars, to name a few. They would go about twice a month. Nancy's favorite part of sk8ing at Rollerena, was doing backward trains, all in synch, jumping to Chic's "Le Freak," "FREAK OUT!" It was awesome!!

Throughout her adulthood she always knew she would come back to Skating. In the early 1980s, Peck and Goode created her 1st Riedell setup. Unfortunately, at the time, there was a death in the family and she lost her skates due to estate politics. Very sad indeed! On November 3,1994, she created her 2nd sk8 set up. They were created at Interskate 88 in Oneonta, NY! To this day she still has the receipt and the name of the person who put them together, Marie Reardon! Funny thing is, she didn't start wearing those second pair of skates until mid to late 2017, when she first went to Brooklyn skates for the first time.

Before the pandemic, Nancy had a thriving holistic practice, teaching folks how to care for their digestive system and improve their health through proper nutrition. Now, her goal is to teach rollerskating as a form of physical fitness and fun.

Over the past 4 years, she relearned how to sk8 and surpassed her sk8 goals, launched a Bronx based sk8 business, @sk8swagnyc, selling jewelry, accessories and sk8wear. and on her way to being a certified skate instructor. One of Nancys' accomplishments is being a Samba dancer and percussionist for a Brooklyn based Brazilian musical group, called, Samba Novo.

She has been performing with them for over 30 years. One of Nancys' goals, was to learn to samba on rollerskates and it took her 1 year to become proficient. Nancys' biggest accomplishment is being a parent to a son who also skates(aggressive inline)!

Since Nancy considers herself a sk8 advocate, one of her current accomplishments is helping to create and facilitate free sk8 events in the Bronx, this past summer, with Chelle Pollard of Sk8Infonetwork! She also uses her Instagram page @bxsk8nyc to promote, inform, educate and celebrate, everything about NYC rollerskating rinks, history of rollerskating, current skate parties, skaters and general sk8 info. Stay tuned, more to come! #longlivesk8ing

On Social Media

FACEBOOK: Nancy Nacim Valdes

INSTAGRAM:

bxsk8nyc

sk8swagnyc

truebeing1

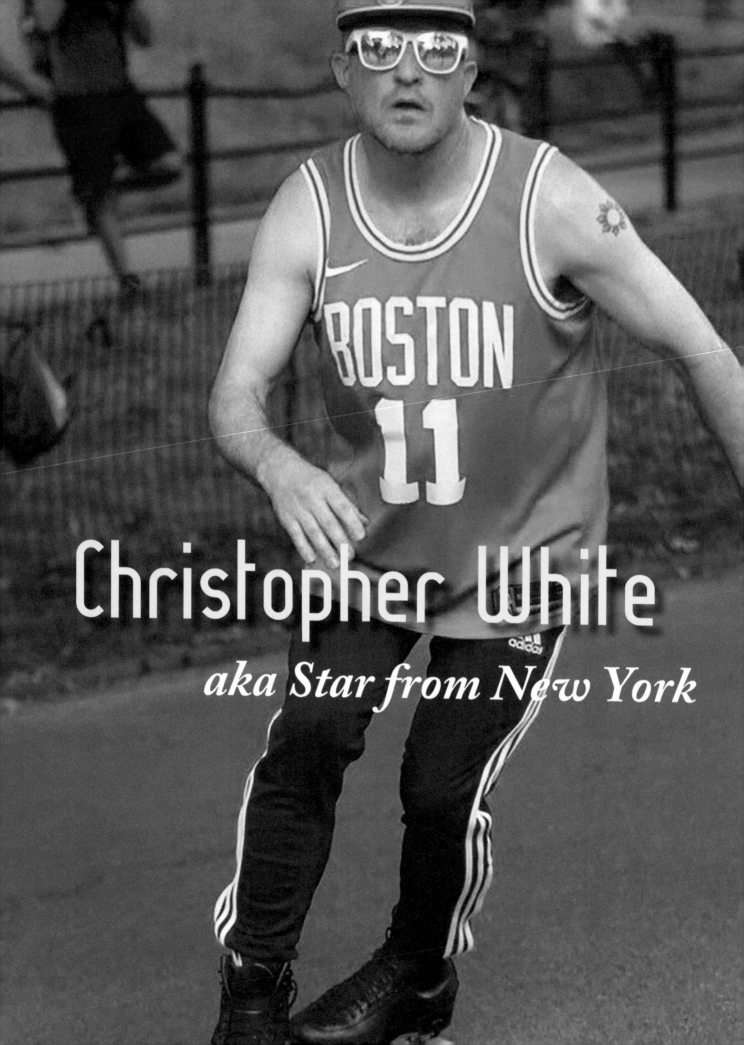

Christopher White

aka Star from New York

What is your skate style?

Philly, house style

What is your skate setup?

Black Reidell Quads, Roll Line Spin NTS Plates, White Wheels

What is your favorite skate song?

"Baby, Be Mine" by Michael Jackson

The very first time you laced up, how did you feel?

I was a skateboarder for many years so I always loved being on wheels, but the first time I laced up and jammed out on skates to amazing dance music, I felt so free and just truly happy.

What are your hidden superpowers, something crazy unique—secret power—that others don't know about you?

My secret power is my ability to keep a beat and do line dancing routines. I love solo skating, but the energy I get when I'm skating in formation with other people pushes me even more to just skate my hardest.

Do you feel you inspire others when you skate?

Yes! Especially when a song I love comes on and we're doing one of my favorite line dance routines. My energy is contagious!

How has skating impacted your life?

For me, sk8ing is a musical, spiritual, skating is my primary emotional release from the stress of life. I let go of all of my worries about business and money and such when I'm skating. I can't wait to skate!

What would you like your legacy to be?

I want to be remembered as someone who loved taking beautiful dance music and taking the raw emotional power from the music and transferring that to skating.

CHRIS WHITE is a New Jersey native who had the opportunity to learn from amazing skaters in Philadelphia such as Master J, Irvin Williams, and Terminator Tex. Chris has been residing in Brooklyn, New York, for the last 10 years and runs his own creative digital agency called Sneakers. His home skating spot is Central Park as part of the Central Park Dance Skaters Association. Whether holding down with the line dancers or jamming out solo style, you'll know that Chris is one white boy who has some serious SOUL!

On Social Media

FACEBOOK:

mrchristopher124

INSTAGRAM:

mrchristopher124

Samuel Raphael Franco

aka Sammy Dees from New York

What is your skate style?

Freestyle, Artistic/Expressionist

What is your skate setup?

Bont Carbon Hybrid, Pilot Falcon Plate, Rusty Old Bearings

What is your favorite skate song?

"Darling Nikki," by Prince

The very first time you laced up, how did you feel?

Felt amazing. I was surrounded by the happiest community in Golden Gate Park and I felt the magic around me. People of all ages, styles, and backgrounds. I felt like I was at home.

What are your hidden superpowers, something crazy unique—secret power—that others don't know about you?

Other than my happy feet, I have magic hands and do bodywork and rehabilitation as a physical therapist in addition to my skate performing work.

I am also a closet assassin with a mean streak on the roller derby track.

Do you feel you inspire others when you skate?

I certainly hope so. There is a picture from skate love Barcelona with some children of skaters enraptured by my performance and I hope I can make everyone else feel that way. I feel like I've inspired many of my friends to strap on a pair of skates and change their lives for the better.

How has skating impacted your life?

It has saved my life, bar none. I was addicted to Opiates in my early 20s, and skating gave me a second family that supported me as I got clean, rebuilt my body, and went back to school. Trying to be a champion with the New York Stock Exchange gave me the kick in the butt to move back to New York and refocus my life as I also earned my Doctorate in Physical Therapy. But beyond that ,all of the friends that I made from skating in California, New York, and now across the world is a community that I will always have and cherish.

Over the last decade I've skated around the world coaching roller derby and teaching dance skating in Puerto Rico, Israel, Ireland, France, the UK, Spain, Australia and hope-fully many more places. Wherever I go, skaters are blood to me.

What would you like your legacy to be?

I want to be remembered as someone who lived free, spread love, and made folks laugh and smile. Maybe even bought them a drink or two and turned them on ;)

SAMUEL RAPHAEL FRANCO has worked as a skate dance performer for 13 years, including featured performances at Skate Love Barcelona, Paris on Wheelz, and as a resident performer at NYC's Dreamland Rollerdisco. In addition to his disco pursuits, Sammy is a world champion and 4-time international medalist in Men's Roller Derby with the New York Shock Exchange. Off skates, you can find him treating patients as a Doctor of Physical Therapy, making people laugh as a stand up comedian, and making men and women swoon at karaoke bars across the world.

On Social Media

FACEBOOK: samuelraphael

INSTAGRAM: samydees

Dr. Carrie Cameron

*aka Sk8Pastor from
New York and North Carolina*

What is your skate style?
Freestyle

What is your skate setup?
VNLA Godfather Fame Indoor boot with Sure Grip Wheels

What is your favorite skate song?
"Gotta Be Funky"

The very first time you laced up, how did you feel?
The first time I laced up, it felt like I was going to fly.

What are your hidden superpowers, something crazy unique—secret power—that others don't know about you?
I can write backwards, so people can't read my notes.

Do you feel you inspire others when you skate?
Yes, I speak the gospel of Jesus while on my skates.

How has skating impacted your life?
Skating impacted my life by falling down. No matter how many times we fall you must get up and keep on rolling.

What would you like your legacy to be?
Loving God, loving people and sk8ing.

DR. CARRIE CAMERON is a born again believer in Jesus Christ from NYC, and the Founder of Upper Room Theological University Inc. Accreditation 1st African American Lady in Fayetteville, North Carolina.

On Social Media

FACEBOOK: Carrie Cameron

Julio Martinez

aka Duce Martinez from New Jersey

What is your skate style?

My skate style is more like Freestyle.

What is your skate setup?

My skate setup is a quad, Riedel 220, Century, Flomax

What is your favorite skate song?

Well, there a few to choose from, but here are my top three:

1. "First Choice" by Dr. Love
2. "Love Is A Message" by Mfsb
3. "Here Comes The Express" by BT Express

The very first time you laced up, how did you feel?

The very first time I laced up was when I lived in Spanish Harlem (El Barrio). That's uptown east side Manhattan.

My cousins were skaters and I watched them skate up and down 3rd Avenue, especially my cousin Ruben Alvarez, who was a badass on skates. He was smooth and, of course, the ladies loved him. I wanted to be like him. So I asked him to teach me, so he did. We went to get plates, wheels and boots, but I decided to use Pro Keds high top sneakers instead. *Yes*, we made our own skates, and they were the *ish*! I laced them up and I felt like Clark Kent when he went into the phone booth and transformed into a superhero. So I felt like a superhero: "DuceyHero!"

What are your hidden superpowers, something crazy unique—secret power—that others don't know about you?

My hidden superpowers that no one knew about was break dancing on skates. My secret power move was doing head spins and windmills while having my skates on, No one could beat that!

Do you feel you inspire others when you skate?

I believe so. When I skate, my energy and skate skills brought skaters together to dance. It was magical.

How has skating impacted your life?

It impacted my life in so many ways where it became the start of my career as a break dancer for one of New York's top three dance crews (Dynamic Rockers to then forming Dynamic Breakers). I took my skate skills from wheels to the floor and I became a well-known dancer (Dynamic Breaker).

We entered one of the biggest break dance contests that was televised on channel 7 ABC in New York City Called "The Big Break Dance Contest" which we won.

Some of the movies and shows we were in, were: *The Last Dragon*, *Fast Forward*, *That's Dancing*, with the late Gene Kelly, *That's Incredible*, *The New Show*, which aired on NBC with Penny Marshall and Rick James.

Skating gave me the ability to put music together for the crew. So I became the DJ and did mix tapes for our shows. We landed the *first* ever hip-hop, 52-city tour that was sponsored by Swatch Watch in the eighties called "The Fresh Fest Tour" with legendary artists like Run DMC, Whodini, Grand Master Flash and the Furious Five, UTFO, Kurtis Blow, The Fat Boys, Newcleus, and many more.

Now from those skating days, I now produce, engineer, promote, have my own record label, and have an Internet radio station called Dwild Music Radio, which is global and with over two million listens: www.dwildmusicradio.com

So this is how skating impacted my life!

What would you like your legacy to be?

As a wonderful and happy person that loved to help others.

On Social Media

FACEBOOK: Duce Martinez

INSTAGRAM: Duce Martinez

YOUTUBE: Duce Martinez

Duce Martinez originally from Spanish Harlem and now living in Newark, New Jersey, has accomplished so many things—from a roller skater to a bboy (Dynamic Rockers/Breakers) to a music producer/music engineer to an international deejay to having his own worldwide Internet radio station (www.dwildmusicradio.com) to now promoting major events. Everyone knows that he is a wild and crazy guy. He is full of life and enjoys putting smiles on people's faces. In other words, there are no secrets!

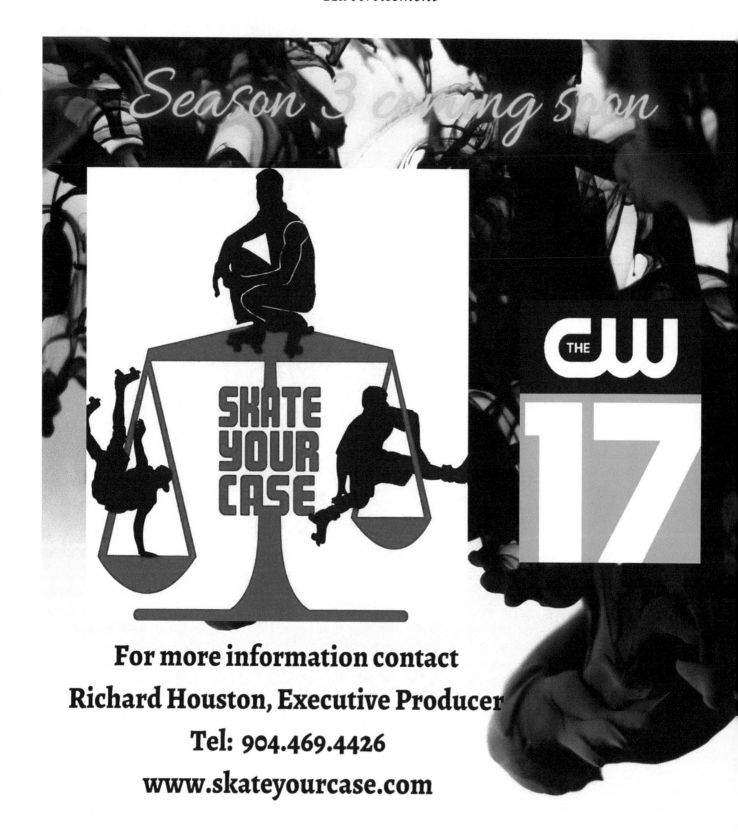

9 781737 846154